All Things
Through Christ

The Ten Most Powerful Words
You Will Ever Understand

Paul Chappell

Striving Together Publications
4020 E. Lancaster Blvd.
Lancaster, CA 93535
800.201.7748

Edited by Cary Schmidt and Maggie Ruhl
Cover design by Jeremy Lofgren
Layout by Craig Parker

ISBN 1-59894-014-7

Printed in the United States of America

Table of Contents

Introduction

Do you know who the world's best author is? His book has been the top seller since its words were penned. Although He has only written *one* piece of non-fiction, His fame spreads through generations.

No author has surpassed Him; no skeptic has demolished His work. He wrote a book entitled, *The Holy Bible.* This book has stood against the test of time, the diatribe of critics, the sarcasm of enemies, the questioning of scholars, and the competition of the devil.

Test His authorship. I dare you. Nobody has written like Him, and nobody ever will.

Allow me to prove His ingenuity. Ten words—God, the Author, used ten simple words to communicate what men have taken volumes to write. Within these ten words, God opens the door to promise, faith and application.

Here is an assignment to test *your* writing skills: In ten words, describe your abilities, your source of strength, and your accomplishments in life.

Can you do it? Our human minds cannot put into words what God's wisdom bound into one sentence! These ten words—are easy to read—no hard pronunciations, no long syllables. Yet, they are ten of the most amazing words you will ever ponder:

> *I can do all things through Christ which strengtheneth me.*

Do you realize the magnitude of God's greatness in this sentence? These simple words explode into small intakes of truth. God's profundity forces our minds to chew on God's truth in small bites. Consider each "bite" a different point of view.

Read these ten words aloud and emphasize the bold phrase. Notice when you emphasize each phrase, a different viewpoint to this one sentence is revealed.

I can do all things *through Christ which strengtheneth me.*

I can do all things **through Christ** *which strengtheneth me.*

I can do all things through Christ **which strengtheneth me.**

Each phrase emphasizes a different view of the whole sentence. Just as this exercise brings out the different views, so this book will bring out different viewpoints to God's profound, ten-word sentence. Together, in the coming pages, we will dissect this powerful and profound promise and discover how its truth will change our lives. We will look at it through three separate perspectives.

First, we will look at these ten words as a promise from our Lord. Next, we will learn how the essence of our faith is instilled into this verse. Our third perspective will help us understand the daily confidence that Christ desires to give every believer.

Before reading further, would you open your heart and ask God to use this promise in your life? Ask God to reveal Himself to you and to change you through the principles and applications of this wonderful verse of Scripture.

CHAPTER ONE

A Proclaimed Promise

Weddings are joyous occasions! Life's most cherished and sacred vows are those spoken on a wedding day. When a husband promises to love and cherish his wife, and when a wife promises to love and honor her husband, they are uniting together to fulfill a life of harmony. Together, they are proclaiming their promises to one another.

In the same way, through this verse, God is proclaiming a powerful promise to His children, and He is inviting us to unite with Him in a life of purpose and strength. Notice the characteristics of this promise.

Claiming a Positive Promise

I can do all things through Christ which strengtheneth me.—PHILIPPIANS 4:13

When we look at this verse as a promise, it gives us hope. God promises us that we *can*! No more feeling inadequate! No more feeling unworthy! No more feeling overwhelmed! God's everlasting promise is that we are capable! Where He calls us, He will enable us!

"I Can Do All Things" through Burdens

Not that I speak in respect of want: for I have learned, in whatsoever state I am, therewith to be content. I know both how to be abased, and I know how to abound: every where and in all things I am instructed both to be full and to be hungry, both to abound and to suffer need.—PHILIPPIANS 4:11–12

Chained to a Roman guard as he was imprisoned for Christ, Paul faced many burdens and times of difficulty, yet he learned to be content. He learned that Christ was his sustenance and sufficiency.

Contentment during times of burden and trial is predominantly a Christian grace. It is only known by the child of God who is in love with Christ. Paul was a contented man because he loved Jesus Christ and followed His Cross.

This portion of Scripture categorizes his burdens in two ways: abasement and affliction.

Abasement is not a reference to the place located below a house. The word *abased* means "to bring low, to bring to the ground." Have you ever had a time in your life when you were brought low or when you felt alone and discouraged? Paul said, "I know what it's like to be there." In 2 Corinthians 4:8–10 he wrote, "*We are troubled on every side, yet not distressed; we are perplexed, but not in despair; Persecuted, but not forsaken; cast down, but not destroyed; Always bearing about in the body the dying of the Lord Jesus, that the life also of Jesus might be made manifest in our body.*"

Paul knew what it was like to be discouraged, brought down, and made low. He understood feelings of rejection. He could relate with feelings of inadequacy and unworthiness. His testimony is real to us, because we experience these same feelings today.

Adoniram Judson was one of the great Baptist missionaries of the nineteenth century. In the late 1800s, he went to Burma—a country with no Gospel witness. He worked hard to learn the language and to diligently spread God's Word. He labored for seven consecutive years before he saw his first convert come to Christ. His first wife died, and his second wife became very sick and was placed on a ship and where she later died on her way back to America. On one occasion, he was imprisoned for his faith, yet through all of these trials, he remained faithful. He believed all things were possible through Christ. By the time Adoniram Judson left Burma, there were thousands of Burmese people who had trusted in Jesus Christ because of one man who learned to continue trusting God through his abasement.

Paul not only faced the burden of abasement; he also faced the burden of affliction. He said in Philippians 4:14, *"Notwithstanding ye have well done, that ye did communicate with my affliction."* This word *affliction* means "a pressure or a pain, as in child birth."

One of the famous Baptist preachers in world history, Charles Haddon Spurgeon, had a verse on his bedroom wall hanging just above his bed. The last thing he saw every evening, and the first thing he saw every morning was Isaiah 48:10, which says, *"Behold, I have refined thee, but not with silver; I have chosen thee in the furnace of affliction."* Spurgeon said, "God's choice makes chosen men choice men. We are chosen not in the palace but in the furnace." Spurgeon learned to walk with God during difficult times, and because of this, God used his life greatly.

"I Can Do All Things" through Blessings

God not only gives the victory through burdens, He also brings victory during the blessings of life. Not every day in Paul's life was difficult, though many were. He did experience times of blessing. Paul tells us, *"I know how to abound…But I rejoiced in the Lord greatly, that now at the last your care of me hath flourished again; wherein ye were also careful, but ye lacked opportunity."*

The word *flourish* means "to revive." Paul experienced times of great encouragement and times of abundant flourishing through Christ.

Sometimes, blessing is as great a test as adversity. God is interested in how you respond to times of success. I hope you can say, like the Apostle Paul, "No matter what the season, I can do all things through Christ." Honor Christ in every circumstance.

This positive promise of God can be applied to every season of life. I can do all things through Christ—through seasons of burdens and seasons of blessings.

Rejoice friend! You can be faithful! You can be fruitful! You can—through Christ!

Claiming a Powerful Promise

> *I can do all things **through Christ** which strengtheneth me.*—PHILIPPIANS 4:13

While we can live for Christ and not falter, the second aspect of this verse promises the underlying power that comes from Christ alone. Through Christ, we have access to the power of this promise. He gives us His power in two primary ways.

He Gives His Power through Redemption

A wealthy English family once invited friends to spend some time at their beautiful estate. The happy gathering was almost plunged into a terrible tragedy on the first day. As the children were swimming, one of them went too deep and began to drown. Fortunately, the gardener heard the others screaming and plunged into the pool to rescue the helpless victim. That youngster was Winston Churchill.

His parents, who were deeply grateful to the gardener, asked what they could do to reward him.

He hesitated, and then said, "I wish my son could go to college someday and become a doctor."

"We'll pay his way," replied Churchill's parents.

Years later, when Sir Winston Churchill was prime minister of England, he was stricken with pneumonia. Greatly concerned, the king summoned the best physician that could be found to the bedside of the ailing leader. That doctor was Sir Alexander Fleming, the developer of penicillin. He was also the son of that gardener who had saved Winston from drowning as a boy!

Later Churchill said, "Rarely has one man owed his life twice to the same person."

What was rare in the case of that great English statesman is, in a much deeper sense, a wonderful reality for every believer in Christ. The Heavenly Father has given us the gift of physical life, and through His Son, the Great Physician, He has imparted to us eternal life.

May the awareness that we are doubly indebted to God as our Creator and Redeemer motivate us to present our bodies a living sacrifice, holy and acceptable unto Him.[1]

Redemption comes from Christ alone. There is one way that our sins are forgiven, and that one way is through the blood of Jesus Christ. Hebrews 9:22 says, *"And almost all things are by the law purged with blood; and without shedding of blood is no remission."*

How does strength come from redemption? Scripture answers this question. Isaiah 43:1 says, *"But now thus saith the LORD that created thee, O Jacob, and he that formed thee, O Israel, Fear not: for I have redeemed thee, I have called thee by thy name; thou art mine."*

When we are redeemed, we become God's child. We stand underneath His umbrella of safety. We do not stand alone in the daily spiritual battle, for He fights our enemy through us. We have no reason to worry! If you have been redeemed, Christ is yours, and He is all you need.

He Gives His Power through Renewal

The moment Christ redeems us, He gives us His power through a lifelong process of renewal. This process takes place through the presence of Christ in our lives. When we accept Him into our hearts, we are born again by the Spirit of God, and He takes up residence in our lives. The Bible tells us in John 3:6–7, *"That which is born of the flesh is flesh; and that which is born of the Spirit is spirit. Marvel not that I said unto thee, Ye must be born again."*

Day by day, the power of Christ is renewing, transforming, and changing us into His image. His power is always at work in us and through us, and the more we become like Him, the more He will be seen through us!

A young man enlisted into the military, and was sent to his regiment. The first night, he was in the barracks with about fifteen other young men, who passed the time playing cards and gambling. Before retiring, he fell on his knees and prayed. They began to curse him, jeer at him, and throw boots at him. So it went on the next night and the next. Finally, the young man told the chaplain what had taken place and asked what he should do.

"Well," said the chaplain, "you are not at home now, and the other men have just as much right to the barracks as you have. It makes them mad to hear you pray, and the Lord will hear you just as well if you say your prayers in bed and don't provoke them."

For several weeks the chaplain did not see the young man again, but one day he met him, and asked, "By the way, did you take my advice?"

"I did, for two or three nights."

"How did it work?"

"Well," said the young man, "I felt like a whipped hound, so the third night, I got out of bed, knelt down and prayed."

"Well," asked the chaplain, "How did that work?"

The young soldier answered: "We have a prayer meeting there now every night, and three have been converted. We are praying for the rest."[2]

This young man understood the power of a renewed life! As Christ renews your life, you will not be able to hide His strength and presence. His hand will be evident and His presence in your life will be irresistible.

Claiming a Permanent Promise

*I can do all things through Christ **which strengtheneth me.**—*PHILIPPIANS 4:13

This promise is not temporary! It is a promise for yesterday, today, tomorrow, and for all of eternity. The strength of Christ is continuous. *Strength* means "to endure with power or to make strong." We don't have to worry about the strength of Christ ever waning or about this promise ever faltering. We are continually made strong with Christ!

> *But they that wait upon the LORD shall renew their strength; they shall mount up with wings as eagles; they shall run, and not be weary; and they shall walk, and not faint.*—ISAIAH 40:31

We all become weary from time to time. We grow weak and become discouraged. Yet, God's promise remains true and waits to be claimed. His promise is eternal and will never fail!

How does God impart this strength to us practically? I believe Christ's strength comes through several different God-given conduits.

God Gives Strength through the Preaching of His Word

Jonathan Edwards was a brilliant theologian whose sermons had an overwhelming impact on those who heard him. His famous sermon, "Sinners in the Hands of an Angry God," moved hundreds to repentance and sparked a revival known as "The Great Awakening."

From a human standpoint, it seems unbelievable that such far-reaching results could come from one message. Edwards did not have a commanding voice or eloquent speech. He used very few gestures, and, he read from a manuscript. Yet, God's Spirit moved upon his hearers with conviction and power.

One message, one Bible, one man of God, one service—these were the ingredients of changed lives. What if the sermon you deliberately missed was meant to change your entire life for the better? We need the consistent preaching of God's Word.

Few know the spiritual preparation involved in the sermon, "Sinners in the Hands of an Angry God." John Chapman gives us the story: "For three days, Edwards had not eaten a mouthful of food; for three nights he had not closed his eyes in sleep. Over and over again he was heard to pray, 'O Lord, give me New England! Give me New England!' When he arose from his knees and made his way into the pulpit that Sunday, he looked as if he had been gazing straight into the face of God. Even before he began to speak, tremendous conviction fell upon his audience."

Jonathan Edward's congregation drew strength from his powerful preaching. They grew in the knowledge of God by listening to sermons that were empowered by God. It is through a man of God expounding on Scriptures that our hearts and eyes open to truths and our lives are strengthened in the grace of God.

> *Thou art my hiding place and my shield: I hope in thy word…Uphold me according unto thy word, that I may live: and let me not be ashamed of my hope.*—Psalm 119: 114, 116

Friend, if you find your spiritual strength faltering, dive into the Word of God! Fill your heart and life with the fresh water of Bible preaching. God will renew your strength through the preaching of His Word.

God Gives Strength through the People of God

Naomi experienced overwhelming loss when her husband and two sons passed away. She felt the hand of God depart from her. Bitterness overcame her steady mind, and she wanted to be alone. She urged her two daughters-in-law to return to their homeland, a place where they could start over. She pleaded with them to leave and told them she had no hope to offer.

Ruth, knowing she would give up her family, her chance of remarrying, and her joy of having children, clave to Naomi. Through this time of sorrow, these two women drew strength from one another. They were women of God. They comforted one another as they grew through their circumstances in life. In the end, God gave Ruth a husband named Boaz, and Naomi became a grandmother to a boy named Obed, the father of Jesse, the grandfather of David.

These two women did exactly what we are commanded to do. First Thessalonians 5:11 says, *"Wherefore comfort yourselves together, and edify one another, even as also ye do."* God calls His people to a strengthening, encouraging, edifying relationship with one another through the local church. It is His will that we gather together and encourage one another. He will use the local body of Christ to give us His strength and power.

He commands us in Hebrews 10:24–25 to faithfully be a part of this local body where we will be "provoked" to love and good works. *"And let us consider one another to provoke unto love and to good works: Not forsaking the assembling of ourselves together, as the manner of some is; but exhorting one another: and so much the more, as ye see the day approaching."*

Consider those with whom you choose to spend with. Are they Christians, committed to Christ? Do you relate with them because of the common spiritual ground you share in Christ? The purpose of fellowship is to draw strength from the people of God. We have been given to each other as a family, and God desires our relationships with fellow Christians to be encouraging and strengthening through His Spirit.

When God gave us these ten words, He proclaimed a powerful, positive, and permanent promise! Friend, think on these words:

> *I can do all things through Christ which strengtheneth me.*

What are you facing that seems insurmountable? What burden are you bearing? What mountain must you cross? What need do you have?

Claim God's promise right now—you *can* accomplish His will for your life!

CHAPTER TWO

A Powerful Faith

The second perspective on this verse explains the essence of our faith. These words give us a blueprint for our belief. They open the door of understanding by describing the Christian faith in one simple sentence.

I can do all things through Christ which strengtheneth me.

The Spirit of Our Faith

I can do all things through Christ which strengtheneth me.—PHILIPPIANS 4:13

When I had the opportunity to come to the city of Lancaster to begin serving as pastor, I sought the counsel of some pastors. I'll never forget what one of them said to me. He said, "Well, if you go to Lancaster, there's only one way to go from there, and that's up, because there's not much going on there." Often, I am reminded of the words of Dr. Tom Malone, "When God is going to do something miraculous, He starts with the impossible."

God is looking for people who still believe that God can. Someone once said, "Whether you think you can or not, you're right." If you think you can, you can. If you think you can't, then you're right—you probably can't.

The same is true with our God. He responds to our belief. If we have faith, believing He can—He will. If we do not believe He can—He won't! Yet, the God who gave us this promise still *can*! The question is this: will you believe? Will you claim the faith embodied in this verse as your very own?

This steadfast faith was at the heart of the Apostle Paul's ministry. Paul displayed his spirit in two ways: he was positive and productive in his spirit of faith.

Our Faith Gives Us a Positive Spirit

Paul said *"I can!"* If you and I are Christians filled with faith, we will have a positive spirit. Even though God promises we *can*, He desires for us to have the right spirit towards Him, no matter what assignment He gives to us.

If God called you to be a janitor, you would probably not doubt your ability to pick up trash. However, would your spirit be positive? When Paul wrote, *"I can do…"* his spirit was positive about whatever God gave him to do! Paul wasn't concerned about status or fame. He wasn't concerned about self-promotion or a paycheck. He wasn't looking for any particular assignment from God. He was only concerned about serving Christ and doing whatever God called him to do. Paul was saying, "No matter what God gives me to do, I can do it through Christ!" What a great attitude!

Paul was compassionate for others.

Paul's spirit was so positive that no matter what he experienced, he maintained a compassion for others. When Paul went to Philippi to preach the Gospel, he reached his first convert, a businesswoman named Lydia. Shortly after, he was thrown into jail

for preaching the Gospel and reaching lost souls in
Philippi.

> *And when they had laid many stripes upon*
> *them, they cast them into prison, charging*
> *the jailor to keep them safely: Who, having*
> *received such a charge, thrust them into the*
> *inner prison, and made their feet fast in*
> *the stocks. And at midnight Paul and Silas*
> *prayed, and sang praises unto God: and the*
> *prisoners heard them.*—ACTS 16:23–25

Did you notice that last verse? At midnight, Paul
and Silas prayed and sang praises to God. Wow! Talk
about a man with a positive spirit! Imagine yourself
in a dark, cold, wet prison singing praises to God.
They possessed something we all need—a positive
faith in God.

In his commentary on Philippians, F. B. Meyer
wrote of the contentment that came as Paul remained
compassionate for the Lord.

> Where shall we find it? Where barns are
> full of grain and the sheds of cattle, where
> mansions overlook miles of parkland
> and landscape, where the feet sink ankle-

deep into the rich piles of carpets, and upholsterers have done their utmost to furnish the rooms with dazzling elegance, where the murmur of the outer world hardly enters, and where distracting care has no twig of which to perch, not there. When every human life is surrounded by every circumstance of comfort and luxury, it is very often the fullest of complaining and discontent. If we would find contentment, let us go to homes where women are crippled with rheumatism or dying of cancer, where comforts are few, where long hours of loneliness are not broken by the intrusion of friendly faces, where the pittance of public charity hardly suffices for necessary needs, to say nothing of comfort. It is there that contentment reveals itself like a shy flower. How often in the homes of the wealthy one has missed it, to find it in the homes of the poor. How often it is wanting where health is buoyant to be discovered, where disease is wearing out the strength. So it is with the apostle, who is in the saddest part of his career, bound to a Roman soldier, enclosed in some narrow apartment, in touch with only a few friends who made no effort to discover him, away from the happier scenes of earlier years. Anticipating Nero's bar, he breaks out into these glorious expressions. He had learned how to be abased in the valley of the shadow, he wore the flower in his buttonhole.

After pastoring for twenty years, I find the people with the greatest complaints and most depressing complexes are those who have health, cars, homes, children, and well-paying jobs. Many times, the Christians with the most positive spirit also have the greatest burdens.

Dora Craig, a wonderful woman in our church who has various health burdens, lives in a convalescent hospital and must depend on someone to bring her to church. She has never uttered one complaint to me. Her words always amaze me, because they are filled with encouragement and comfort. It is only through Christ that Dora Craig lives with such a positive outlook on life.

I remember vividly the night that I visited another dear lady from our church family, Mary Holder. Her body was filled with cancer, and she was suffering great discomfort. As I entered that room, she looked at me with a smile from Heaven and said, "Pastor, I'm so glad you're here. Oh, Pastor, God is so good. I was able to lead my nurse to Christ." Just hours before she slipped off into eternity, she was showing compassion to others.

When the strength of Christ comes into your life, your attitude toward life changes! Your spirit becomes positive in Christ, and that positive spirit overflows with the compassion of Christ.

Paul was confident in the Lord.

Not only was Paul compassionate for the Lord; he was also confident in the Lord. We will look more closely at this confidence in our next section, but notice what Paul said in Philippians 1:6, *"Being confident of this very thing, that he which hath begun a good work in you will perform it until the day of Jesus Christ."*

When things seem astounding, remember that your God is astounding! Have you ever seen the Grand Canyon? Have you considered that He created and placed the stars into space? Do you realize God spoke the universe into existence with words alone? Our God's power is beyond our comprehension, and He deserves nothing less than our complete confidence.

In 1 Samuel 17, David saw the giant, Goliath, cursing his God. He saw his brothers and the men of Israel cowering before this giant. David was a young man who had faith in his almighty God.

Years ago a man left our church and said to me, "I want to tell you right now, you're not even old enough to be an elder."

I replied, "You might be right, but sometimes God will use the faith of a young man." That man was right, I was not old enough to pastor by human standards, but God blesses faith—confidence in Christ! For the past twenty years, he has!

David went to Saul and boldly said, "...*Let no man's heart fail because of him; thy servant will go and fight with this Philistine.*" David told Saul that he would stand and fight the mighty Philistine. Saul replied, "...*Thou art not able to go against this Philistine to fight with him: for thou art but a youth, and he a man of war from his youth.*" In essence, he told David that he wasn't old enough to be a warrior.

David did not give in. He persistently replied, "...*Thy servant kept his father's sheep, and there came a lion, and a bear, and took a lamb out of the flock: And I went out after him, and smote him, and delivered it out of his mouth: and when he arose against me, I caught him by his beard, and smote him, and slew him. Thy servant slew both the lion and the bear: and this uncircumcised Philistine shall be as one of them, seeing he hath defied the armies of the living God. David said moreover, The LORD that delivered me out of the paw of the lion, and out of the paw of the bear, he will deliver me out of the hand of this Philistine. And Saul said unto David, Go, and the LORD be with thee."*

David had a positive spirit of confidence in God. He knew he could not fight Goliath in his own strength. Because of this, he put his complete trust in God, who fought his enemy for him. Study the story of David in 1 Samuel 17. You will never find a time when David's spirit was negative! This is why David is known as a man after God's own heart.

Our Faith Gives Us a Productive Spirit

Henry Ford once said, "You can't build a reputation on what you're *going* to do." Intentions are only thoughts; they mean nothing except to the person who thinks them. Paul understood this truth! He didn't say, "I can *intend* to do…." He was a man of productive action. He said, *"I can **do**…."* I think Paul would have liked that Nike slogan, "Just **Do** It!"

Do you know people who are always busy, but never productive? They are constantly running, but have nothing to show for their busyness! They look very busy, but they never actually *do* anything! Well, that is *not* how the Apostle Paul was. Every time Paul left a city, there was a new church in existence. The people he led to the Lord were being discipled—they were being established, edified, and grounded in the Word of God. Paul clearly states that he was compelled and confident in Christ to *do* what God called him to do. He believed Christ could make him productive in the work that God gave him. He was a man of action, not merely good intentions.

> *For the love of Christ constraineth us;*
> *because we thus judge, that if one died for all,*
> *then were all dead.*—2 CORINTHIANS 5:14

> *Brethren, I count not myself to have*
> *apprehended: but this one thing I do,*
> *forgetting those things which are behind,*
> *and reaching forth unto those things which*
> *are before, I press toward the mark for the*
> *prize of the high calling of God in Christ*
> *Jesus.*—PHILIPPIANS 3:13–14

Paul was constantly pressing on the upward way—positive that God would keep using him. It didn't matter that he was in jail. It didn't matter that he had been forsaken by Demas. It didn't matter that his health was failing and his eyes were weak. It didn't matter that a Roman soldier had him bound. God was not bound, and Paul's confidence remained strong. No matter the circumstance or trial, Paul's faith and confidence in Christ produced a productive spirit. He looked at every circumstance as a God-ordained moment to accomplish something for Christ.

As you grow in the faith embodied in this verse, you will become a Christian of action! Your faith will compel you to live on purpose for a purpose. Your heart will yearn to be productive—to accomplish something for the glory of God.

The Scope of our Faith

*I can **do all things** through Christ which strengtheneth me.*—Philippians 4:13

Paul did not compartmentalize his Christianity. So many Christians dust their Bible off on Sunday, and let it sit on the shelf the rest of the week. The scope of faith for many Christians is limited to about three hours per week.

The faith we see in these powerful ten words is a completely different kind of faith! This faith encompasses all of life. Paul used the words *"all things."* God wants your relationship with Him—your faith—to be the very core of every part of your life. "All things" simply means *all things*!

These two words, *"all things,"* can make our faith personal and practical in our daily lives.

Our Faith Encompasses Our Personal Life

First and foremost, your faith should be personal and should include a daily walk with Christ! Colossians 2:6–7 says, *"As ye have therefore received Christ Jesus the Lord, so walk ye in him: Rooted and built up in him, and stablished in the faith, as ye have been taught, abounding therein with thanksgiving."*

If a husband spent one week without talking to his wife, he would be in big trouble! He would fail in maintaining a close relationship with her. Our relationship with our Heavenly Father is the same. If we go days without talking or conversing with Him, we are failing to cultivate a close relationship with Him.

If you get discouraged about maintaining a consistent time with Christ, you are not alone. Do not let this discouragement control your thinking. God promised that we can do all things. We must simply have faith that, with God, we can!

The scope of our faith should also include our personal witness. Paul desired for his witness to become stronger. This ought to be the prayer of our hearts as well. He stated in Acts 20:19–20: *"Serving the LORD with all humility of mind, and with many tears, and temptations, which befell me by the lying in wait of the Jews: And how I kept back nothing that was profitable unto you, but have shewed you, and have taught you publickly, and from house to house."*

Our walk, our witness—both are possible through Jesus Christ. In the midst of a generation screaming for answers, Christians are stuttering when they ought to be speaking the truth in love and giving answers from Scripture.

R.A. Torrey once said, "There is more joy in Jesus in 24 hours than there is in the world in 365 days. I have tried them both." The world needs Christians with a genuine walk with God and a consistent witness for Him. They long for the joy that can only be found in Christ.

Simply put, when you embrace the dynamic faith found in these ten words, *"I can do **all things** through Christ which strengtheneth me,"* your personal life will be radically different. You will walk with Christ throughout the day. You will view every task, every opportunity, and every person through the eyes of His purpose for your life.

Our Faith Encompasses Our Family Life

Second, our faith should include our family life. God desires for your family to be built upon your faith in Jesus Christ. He wants to be the source of strength and the foundation of your home.

If you are married, this powerful verse brings the strength of Christ into your marriage relationship! It gives you hope that your marriage can grow stronger year by year. You may think, "Well, you don't know who I'm married to." Friend, stop focusing on who you are married to, and start focusing on *Who* is *inside* of you! If Christ reigns in your home, then He intends to give you a strong home! If God brought you together, then He will enable you to stay together.

Through Christ, it is possible for couples to stay married "till death do us part."

When Mark Twain lectured in Utah, a Mormon acquaintance argued with him about polygamy. After a long, heated debate, the Mormon finally asked, "Can you give me one single passage of Scripture that forbids polygamy?"

Mark Twain thought about it, then answered, "Yes, *'No man can serve two masters.'*"

This statement reminds me that in every home there ought to be one Master—the Lord Jesus Christ. Everything about your home should be under the authority of Jesus Christ. When Paul stated, *"I can do all things…"* he was including loving your spouse, nurturing your children, and building a loving family. Allow your faith to encompass your family life and watch God bless your home as a result!

Our Faith Encompasses Our Church Life

Third, our faith should extend to our church life. Your church should be a spiritual church of faith and growth in Christ. The faith found in these words of Philippians 4:13 will compel your church forward in the strength and grace of God.

The Bible says in Philippians 1:27, *"Only let your conversation be as it becometh the gospel of Christ: that whether I come and see you, or else be absent, I may hear of your affairs, that ye stand fast in one spirit, with one mind striving together for the faith of the gospel."* With one Spirit—the Holy Spirit, and with one mind on the Word of God, churches should strive together for the faith of the Gospel.

These ten words will compel you to be faithful in your local church. Through Christ, you can make the local church a priority in your life. When peers at work don't understand, when your boss will not cut you slack, and when your family does not want to get involved, this verse will compel you to take a stand and make church a priority in your life. God said you are capable of doing all things. Attending God's house faithfully is a part of this guarantee. Take it one week at a time. Ask God to help you clear your schedule for what is most important. As He assists you, your faith in Him will grow.

The scope of the faith found in this verse is all encompassing! This faith should be an intricate part of your personal life, your family life, and your church life. That's exactly what Paul meant when he said *"all things."*

The Source of Our Faith

> *I can do all things **through Christ which strengtheneth me.***—Philippians 4:13

When it comes to living by faith, God desires to instruct us, and He has a wealth of knowledge I do not have. Only through Him, I can obtain skills to live a faithful and fruitful Christian life. Just as I relied on the help of others to learn how to drive, I must rely on God alone to live the Christian life.

Paul concludes this verse with these wonderful words, *"...through Christ which strengtheneth me."* You must recognize that Jesus Christ is the source of your faith and your growth in grace. It is not through you; it is all through Christ Who strengthens you.

The attributes of Jesus Christ make Him the all-sufficient source for our faith.

Our Faith Flows from the Attributes of God

A promise of strength is only as good as the source of the promise. When Paul said, *"through Christ,"* he was making a big statement. When you understand who Jesus really is and how limitless His strength is, this

33

verse takes on a whole new context. Just who is this Jesus Christ who strengthens us?

Jesus Christ is omnipotent. He is all-powerful. Revelation 19:6–7 says it this way, *"And I heard as it were the voice of a great multitude, and as the voice of many waters, and as the voice of mighty thunderings, saying, Alleluia: for the Lord God omnipotent reigneth. Let us be glad and rejoice, and give honour to him: for the marriage of the Lamb is come, and his wife hath made herself ready."*

He is omniscient. He is all-knowing. Matthew 12:25 says of Christ, *"And Jesus knew their thoughts, and said unto them, Every kingdom divided against itself is brought to desolation; and every city or house divided against itself shall not stand."*

He is omnipresent. He is everywhere all the time. Matthew 28:20 says, *"...lo, I am with you alway, even unto the end of the world."* Again in John 3:13 the Bible says, *"And no man hath ascended up to heaven, but he that came down from heaven, even the Son of man which is in heaven."*

He is immutable. He does not change. Hebrews 13:8 says, *"Jesus Christ the same yesterday, and to day, and for ever."* What God did yesterday, He can still do today! He never changes.

He is an eternal God. He did not begin his existence in Bethlehem. He was before Bethlehem; He was before Abraham. He was before the beginning of time. He always has been and always will be. John 1:1–2 says, *"In the beginning was the Word, and the Word was with God, and the Word was God. The same was in the beginning with God."*

Referring to Christ's existence, President Ronald Reagan made the following statement:

> Meaning no disrespect to the religious conviction of others, I still can't help wondering how we can explain away what is to me the greatest miracle of all, and which is recorded in history. No one denies there was such a man, and that He lived, and that He was put to death by crucifixion. Where is this miracle spoken of? Well consider this, and let your imagination translate this into your own time, possibly in your own hometown.
>
> A young man whose father is a carpenter grows up working in His father's shop. One day He puts down His tools and walks out of His father's shop. He starts

preaching on street corners and in nearby countryside, walking from place to place preaching all the while, even though He's not an ordained minister. He does this for three years, then He is arrested, tried and convicted. There is no court of appeal, so He is executed at age thirty-three along with two common thieves. Those in charge of His execution roll dice to see who gets His clothing, the only possession He has. His family cannot afford a burial place for Him, so He is interned in a borrowed tomb.

End of story? No. This young man, who left no written word, has for 2,000 years had a greater effect on the world than all the rulers, kings, emperors, all the conquerors, generals, and admirals, all the scholars, scientists, and philosophers, who ever lived. All of them put together. How do we explain that, unless He really was who He said He was?

We serve a living Saviour! He is omnipotent. He is omniscient. He is omnipresent. He is immutable.

He is eternal. He is God, and I can do all things through Him!

Our Faith Flows from the Assistance of God

Paul said, "He strengthens us." God doesn't send you into your journey of faith without help! He walks with you, day by day, assisting and enabling you to do His will.

One of my favorite portions of Scripture is Psalm 23. This passage so powerfully shows how God helps us. It describes the Christ who strengthens us. Whether I read it at a graveside, a bedside, the pulpit, or in my private study, it always blesses my heart. Take a moment to read this passage, and delight once again in how Christ promises to assist you through this life of faith.

> *The LORD is my shepherd; I shall not want. He maketh me to lie down in green pastures: he leadeth me beside the still waters. He restoreth my soul: he leadeth me in the paths of righteousness for his name's sake. Yea, though I walk through the valley of the shadow of death, I will fear no evil: for thou art with me; thy rod and thy staff*

they comfort me. Thou preparest a table before me in the presence of mine enemies: thou anointest my head with oil; my cup runneth over. Surely goodness and mercy shall follow me all the days of my life: and I will dwell in the house of the LORD for ever.—PSALM 23

Jesus Christ provides for us, for He says, *"I shall not want."* When you are so weary you cannot go on, He says He will restore your soul. When it seems as if you are carrying your burdens alone, He says, *"thy rod and thy staff they comfort me."* He protects you when you walk through the valley of the shadow of death. He gives you a special anointing. His rewards lie in His goodness and mercy, and He promises an eternal home with Him.

You are not alone in this faith journey. Christ is your source! He walks with you. He assists you. He sustains you moment by moment. Keep your eyes on Him and your heart close to Him.

These powerful words define a powerful faith. *"I can do all things through Christ which strengtheneth me."* In just ten words, God brings the entire Christian faith into focus.

The spirit of our faith says, *"I can...."* This is a positive, confident spirit!

The scope of our faith says, *"...do all things..."* This encompasses every part of our lives.

The source of our faith says, *"...through Christ which strengtheneth me."* The God of the universe promises us His strength and assistance through every step of our journey!

CHAPTER THREE

A Practical Confidence

Journey with me to yet another vantage point of this powerful verse and see it in one last perspective—a personal, practical perspective. We've seen this verse as a proclaimed promise. We've studied it as a powerful faith. Now let's ask this question. What does this verse produce in the life of the believer who applies it personally?

> *I can do all things through Christ which strengtheneth me.*

William Carey, the great missionary to India in the late 1700s, often said, "Attempt great things for

God and expect great things from God." In his forty-three years living in India, God used him to translate the entire Bible into six languages, the New Testament into twenty languages, and various portions of the Bible into forty languages. Along the way, William Carey brought thousands of people to the Lord Jesus Christ. His life and testimony exemplifying the statement, "Godly courage is ignoring the fear of failure while attempting great things for God."

Christian, if you will personally apply this verse, you, like William Carey will attempt great things for God and expect great things from God.

The Confidence of the Believer

I can do all things through Christ which strengtheneth me.—PHILIPPIANS 4:13

Paul did not say "I hope" things will turn out well. He said. "*I can do all things.*" The phrase, *can do*, is in the present tense which means God's power is continual. Paul relied on God's continual help. This confidence was a disposition placed into his heart by the Holy Spirit. It was a conviction—a mood of certainty in which he lived. He confidently and steadfastly went forward in the faith of Jesus Christ.

This Confidence Is Not a Self-confidence

The confidence of the believer is a "God" confidence. Paul wrote in Philippians 3:4–10, *"Though I might also have confidence in the flesh. If any other man thinketh that he hath whereof he might trust in the flesh, I more: Circumcised the eighth day, of the stock of Israel, of the tribe of Benjamin, an Hebrew of the Hebrews; as touching the law, a Pharisee; Concerning zeal, persecuting the church; touching the righteousness which is in the law, blameless. But what things were gain to me, those I counted loss for Christ. Yea doubtless, and I count all things but loss for the excellency of the knowledge of Christ Jesus my Lord: for whom I have suffered the loss of all things, and do count them but dung, that I may win Christ, And be found in him, not having mine own righteousness, which is of the law, but that which is through the faith of Christ, the righteousness which is of God by faith: That I may know him, and the power of his resurrection, and the fellowship of his sufferings, being made conformable unto his death."*

In these verses, Paul shares his personal testimony. He knew if anybody had bragging rights, it was him. He had the education and the religious training, which elevated his status in society. He was a powerful leader to all those around him. Yet, he knew that the things which gave him credibility in the eyes of men meant nothing in the eyes of God. He counted all his accomplishments but loss. Paul was not a self-confident man; he was a God-confident man.

Confidence in self is, in actuality, reliance upon the flesh and is a sure recipe for spiritual disaster. You cannot live the Christian life in your own strength.

In July, 1911, a man named Bobby Leach went over Niagara Falls in a steel drum and lived to tell about it. Although he suffered minor injuries, he survived. He recognized the tremendous dangers involved in the feat, and he did everything he could to protect himself from harm. He was attentive to even the smallest detail.

Several years after that incident, while skipping down the street in New Zealand, Bobby Leach slipped on an orange peel. He fell and badly fractured his leg. He was taken to a hospital where he later died of complications from that fall. He received a greater injury walking down the street than the injuries he sustained in going over Niagara Falls.

This is a perfect picture of a self-confident Christian. It's only a matter of time before that self-confidence will lead us to a sure fall. It has been said,

"In whatever man does *without* God, he must fail miserably or succeed more miserably."

> *Be strong and courageous, be not afraid nor dismayed for the king of Assyria, nor for all the multitude that is with him: for there be more with us than with him: With him is an arm of flesh; but with us is the LORD our God to help us, and to fight our battles. And the people rested themselves upon the words of Hezekiah king of Judah.*—2 Chronicles 32:7–8

Friend, be sure that you place your full confidence in Christ alone!

This Confidence Is a Sustaining Confidence

In 1966, about a year before he died, the brilliant physicist J. Robert Oppenheimer said, "I am a complete failure!" This man had been the director of the Los Alamos Project, a research team that produced the atomic bomb, and he also served as the head of the Institute for Advanced Study at Princeton. Yet, looking back on his life, he saw all of his achievements as meaningless. When asked about them, he replied, "They leave on the tongue only the taste of ashes."

The number of people who commit suicide after experiencing the fame and fortune of worldly success is astonishing. Multimillionaire George Vanderbilt killed himself by jumping from a hotel window. Lester Hunt, twice governor of Wyoming before being elected to the U.S. Senate, ended his own life. Actress Marilyn Monroe, writer Ernest Hemingway, and athlete Tony Lazzeri represent a host of highly influential and popular people who became so disenchanted with earthly success that they took their own lives.

The world is floundering around, putting their confidence into whatever feels good. What a contrast this verse is against such a discouraging backdrop! A life lived in the confidence of Christ takes on an eternal significance. This verse, when applied to your heart, will breathe fresh vitality into your life and fresh purpose into your steps. This confidence will sustain you through moments of uncertainty, disappointment, and frustration. There is no need to despair if your confidence is in Christ.

What sustains you today? Why did you get out of bed this morning? What are you seeking? Paul had a deep-rooted confidence that sustained him. He put his confidence in Christ for every area of his life.

His confidence was in God's salvation.

In 2 Timothy 1:12 he said, "*For the which cause I also suffer these things: nevertheless I am not ashamed: for I know whom I have believed, and am persuaded that he is able to keep that which I have committed unto him against that day.*"

His confidence was in God's sanctification.

In Philippians 1:6 he said, "*Being confident of this very thing, that he which hath begun a good work in you will perform it until the day of Jesus Christ.*"

His confidence was in God's security.

In Romans 8:38–39 he said, "*For I am persuaded, that neither death, nor life, nor angels, nor principalities, nor powers, nor things present, nor things to come, Nor height, nor depth, nor any other creature, shall be able to separate us from the love of God, which is in Christ Jesus our Lord.*"

His confidence was in God's service and calling.

In 1 Timothy 1:12–14 he said, "*And I thank Christ Jesus our Lord, who hath enabled me, for that he counted me faithful, putting me into the ministry; Who was before a blasphemer, and a persecutor, and injurious: but I obtained mercy, because I did it ignorantly in unbelief. And the grace of our Lord was exceeding abundant with faith and love which is in Christ Jesus."*

In every season and circumstance of Paul's life, God sustained him and gave him confidence. Through imprisonment, beatings, storms and blessings, he had continual confidence in his God, and this confidence sustained him in a way that nothing else could.

Many years ago a man said to me, "It is impossible to follow God without some hurts and heartaches in your life." Perhaps you have experienced this in your life. Remember, mountaintops are where the great views can be seen, but the valleys of life are where the fruit grows. It is during the times of difficulty that God brings forth great lessons that will cause you to bear much fruit.

It doesn't matter who you are, there is a God in Heaven who wants you to have confidence in Him! He is for you! He is on your side! And, He will not give up on you in the middle of your race!

The Companion of the Believer

*I can do all things **through Christ** which strengtheneth me.*—PHILIPPIANS 4:13

Let your conversation be without covetousness;
and be content with such things as ye have:
for he hath said, I will never leave thee, nor
forsake thee. So that we may boldly say, The
Lord is my helper, and I will not fear what
man shall do unto me.—Hebrews 13:5

God designed us for companionship. He created us for fellowship. Every good relationship in our lives, in some way, points to a greater, deeper, and more steadfast relationship that He desires to have personally with us. I'm amazed when I consider this verse in this context—God desires to have a constant companionship with me! My heart delights to think that God is so in love with me, that He desires to accompany me through every circumstance of my life! I say with the psalmist, *"What is man that thou art mindful of him?"* (Psalm 8:4).

Meditate on this thought: Christ is your Companion! You are never alone. You never have to bear a burden, make a decision, face a question, or conquer a temptation in your own strength. You never have to walk alone through this life.

Take comfort in these encouraging characteristics of Christ—your Companion!

Our Companion Is Constant

In Matthew 28, Jesus gathered in Galilee with His disciples and gave to them the Great Commission. Jesus Christ looked into the eyes of His disciples and challenged them to go into the entire world and preach the Gospel. He said in Matthew 28:20, *"Teaching them to observe all things whatsoever I have commanded you: and, lo, I am with you alway, even unto the end of the world."* Knowing they were facing the daunting task of reaching the world with the Gospel, Jesus gave His disciples this amazing promise—*"I am with you alway…."*

G. Campbell Morgan, one of the great British preachers of centuries past, went to a rest home one afternoon. He read the Scriptures to some of the elderly people there. As he was reading God's Word, G. Campbell Morgan came to this passage, *"…lo, I am with you alway even to the end of the world."* He looked at the ladies who were there listening to the Bible reading, and said, "Isn't that a wonderful promise?" In that moment, one of the ladies looked at him and said, "No, that is a wonderful *reality*."

Have you ever felt alone, even in a crowded room? For some people it is easy to slip into a state of loneliness and personal despair. Yet, this kind of self-centered depression is nothing more than a deliberate choice to not acknowledge our constant Companion—Jesus Christ. When loneliness begins to gnaw inside of you, lift up your head and remember that Christ is your constant Companion.

Our Companion Is Concerned

Take this personally—Jesus Christ is concerned for you, and He cares for you. Paul said in 2 Timothy 4:16–17, *"At my first answer no man stood with me, but all men forsook me: I pray God that it may not be laid to their charge. Notwithstanding the Lord stood with me, and strengthened me; that by me the preaching might be fully known, and that all the Gentiles might hear: and I was delivered out of the mouth of the lion."* Jesus is with you right now, and He is acutely aware of and concerned about every detail of your life!

Whether it is the three Hebrew children in a burning, fiery furnace, Daniel in the lion's den, the Apostle Paul on his missionary journey, or *you* tomorrow morning at work—God is concerned for you, and He will stand with you as you stand for Him.

Jackie Robinson was the first black man to play major league baseball. Breaking baseball's color barrier, he faced jeering crowds in every stadium. While playing one day in his home stadium in Brooklyn, he committed an error. Immediately, throughout the stadium, fans began to ridicule him. As the ridicule continued, he stood at second base, humiliated and rejected. Suddenly, shortstop Pee Wee Reese came over and stood next to him. In a moment of rare courage, Reese put his arm around Jackie Robinson and faced the crowd. In that moment, the fans instantly grew quiet. Robinson later said that arm around his shoulder saved his career.

When you're facing a jeering moment in life—when it seems that the devil has unloaded his entire arsenal on your spiritual life—Someone is standing by you! Even when you make an error and Satan condemns you, Jesus Christ comes to your side, shows His wounded hands, and gently places His arm around your shoulder! He is a concerned Companion, and He will never leave your side!

Our Companion Corrects Us

The shepherd's staff was a long wooden rod with a large hook at the end. It was used to rescue sheep that wandered into a position of danger or strayed away from the shepherd. On some occasions, if a sheep was continually wandering, the shepherd would take the staff and break it's leg. Then, set it and carry the sheep until the leg healed. Once the leg mended, the sheep would never leave the shepherd's side.

This may sound harsh or abusive, but it was actually an act of loving correction. It was an act of protection. Allowing the sheep to experience pain was the only path to safety.

An old Jewish proverb says, "A friend is one who warns you." Christ is concerned for us and does stand by us, but out of love, He also warns and corrects us. In Job 5:17, Job said, *"Behold, happy is the man whom God correcteth: therefore despise not thou the chastening of the Almighty."* Proverbs 3:11 says, *"My son, despise not the chastening of the LORD; neither be weary of his correction."*

Friend, God loves you too much to let you wander. As your constant Companion, He will gently nudge you back on to the right path. And yes, sometimes, He may even allow some pain in your life to keep you close to Him. He loves you that much!

The Continuance of the Believer

The Christian life is a marathon. It requires endurance! It requires long-term commitment. Frankly, it requires a kind of steadfastness that we cannot produce ourselves, which begs this question: "How are we going to stay faithful?"

If you have been saved any length of time, you probably know Christians who have fallen away from faithfulness to Christ. You've come this far, but how will you stand strong in the grace of God? How will you keep going when the Christian life becomes difficult? The answer is found in one more look at the last three words of this incredible verse:

> *I can do all things through Christ* **which strengtheneth me.**—PHILIPPIANS 4:13

The word *strengtheneth* is in the present participle, meaning that this strength is given continually to the believer. God is saying in this verse, "I will continually endue you with strength. I will continue to give you fresh strength every day."

The only way you can stay faithful and continue in the Christian life is through the daily strengthening of Jesus Christ. God would not provide strength that you don't need. Accept the fact from this verse that you *continually* need His power. Like a time-release sinus medication, God says His strength is available on a moment-by-moment basis.

Many members of our church have sent loved ones overseas with no assurance of their return. Many have had times when family heartaches were overwhelming and medical questions were many. Through times of questions and uncertainty, I have watched these faithful people stand steadfast in Christ as a testimony of God's continual strength. To each one, God gave His abundant grace moment by moment. His time-released grace was all that was needed in the season of trial or testing.

The Bible says in Isaiah 40:31, "*But they that wait upon the Lord shall renew their strength; they shall mount up with wings as eagles; they shall run, and not be weary; and they shall walk, and not faint.*"

Notice two ways we can possess this wonderful strength in our lives every day.

We Can Continue through the Strength of His Spirit

When I was saved, I was born again by the Holy Spirit. If you are saved, it is because the Holy Spirit convicted you, and you were changed from the inside out. Paul speaks of the Holy Spirit's ministry in 2 Corinthians 4:16, *"For which cause we faint not; but though our outward man perish, yet the inward man is renewed day by day."*

Have you ever had a day when the outward man perishes? Maybe it was a long day of work, dealing with difficult people, or going through the day exhausted. The outward man wants a back rub, a meal, and a good night's rest! The outward man is perishing.

Here is good news: the inward man is renewed day by day. Daily, the Lord gives us joy and strength. He continually reminds us, *"This is the day which the LORD hath made; we will rejoice and be glad in it."* Ephesians 3:16 says, *"That he would grant you, according to the riches of his glory, to be strengthened with might by his Spirit in the inner man:"*

Years ago, some preachers were sitting around a boardroom conference table in the Midwest. They were talking about an upcoming revival meeting and trying to decide which evangelist to invite. One of the older preachers said, "I think we ought to invite D. L. Moody; he's a great man of God." A younger preacher, with a tinge of jealousy in his voice said,

"Why Moody? Does he have a monopoly on the Holy Spirit?" The older preacher looked at the younger preacher and said, "No, but the Holy Spirit has a monopoly on him."

Does the Holy Spirit have a monopoly on you? Have you died to self? Have you sought the fullness of the Spirit? Have you asked God to fill you with His power and grace by the Holy Spirit of God? We can only continue on by the inner strengthening of His Spirit.

We Can Continue through the Strength of His Word

In Psalm 119:114 the psalmist said, *"Thou art my hiding place and my shield: I hope in thy word."* Do you know what the Bible will give to you tomorrow morning, if you open it? It will provide you hope and strength. The news channel and the talk radio will not give you strength, but God's Word will!

In this technological, media-empowered day, we need to be Bible-empowered Christians. Hebrews 4:12 says, *"For the word of God is quick, and powerful, and sharper than any twoedged sword, piercing even to the dividing asunder of soul and spirit, and of the joints and marrow, and is a discerner of the thoughts and intents of the heart."*

D. L. Moody said, "I prayed for faith and it did not come. But I read the Word of God and faith came." Some people look at great tasks, such as building a church, healing a marriage, or mending a family, and they believe they are possible. Quite simply, they are people of the Book. Faith has come into their heart, because God's Word has placed it there!

Ten words—ten powerful, God-inspired words—are God's gift to you. These words give you personal confidence, a constant Companion, and the strength to continue faithfully for God. No matter what you're facing right now, God's words will change your perspective if you will allow the Holy Spirit to apply them to your heart.

Conclusion

Now, do you realize the greatness of this one sentence? Can you stand in awe of God's supreme authorship, now that you have seen what He can do with ten words? Allow these three perspectives to sink deep into your heart and grow into your life.

God proclaims His promise to me—*"I can do all things through Christ which strengtheneth me."*

God defines the entire Christian faith—*"I can do all things through Christ which strengtheneth me."*

God gives me personal confidence and companionship—*"I can do all things through Christ which strengtheneth me."*

Someone once said, "You are who God says you are, and you can do what God says you can do." We are in Christ and we can do all things through Him. What more do we need?

Notes

Chapter One
1. *Our Daily Bread*, April 29, Bible.org.
2. *Moody's Anecdotes*, page 73–74, Bible.org.

For more information about our ministry visit the following websites:

www.strivingtogether.com
for helpful Christian resources

www.dailyintheword.org
for an encouraging word each day

www.lancasterbaptist.org
for information about Lancaster Baptist Church

www.wcbc.edu
for information about West Coast Baptist College